# Hiding the Word
the Attributes of God

A Scripture Memorization Program
Marji Laine Clubine

*HIDING THE WORD: the Attributes of God*

© Copyright 2023 Marji Laine Clubine

ISBN: 978-1-951602-24-6

All rights reserved. No part of this publication may be reproduced or transmitted in any form or by any means without written permission from the publisher.

Published by:

Faith Driven Book Production Services
PO Box 702852
Dallas, TX 75370

Printed in the United States of America

Unless otherwise indicated, all Scripture quotations are taken from the *New American Standard Bible*, Copyright 1960, 1971, 1977, 1995 by The Lockman Foundation. Used by permission. All rights reserved.

Scripture marked as NIV taken from the HOLY BIBLE, NEW INTERNATIONAL VERSION®. NIV®. Copyright © 1973, 1978, 1984 by International Bible Society. Used by permission of Zondervan. All rights reserved worldwide.

Scripture quotations marked (ESV) are from The ESV® Bible (The Holy Bible, English Standard Version®), © 2001 by Crossway, a publishing ministry of Good News Publishers. Used by permission. All rights reserved.

Scripture quotations marked (NLT) are taken from the *Holy Bible*, New Living Translation, copyright ©1996, 2004, 2015 by Tyndale House Foundation. Used by permission of Tyndale House Publishers, Carol Stream, Illinois 60188. All rights reserved.

Scripture marked ASV from the American Standard Version and those marked KJV from the King James Version are public domain.

Scripture marked NKJV taken from the NEW KING JAMES VERSION Copyright© 1982 by Thomas Nelson, Inc. Used by permission. All rights reserved.

Scripture marked BSB from The Holy Bible, Berean Standard Bible, produced in cooperation with Bible Hub, Discovery Bible, OpenBible.com, and the Berean Bible Translation Committee. This text of God's Word has been dedicated to the public domain.

# Dedication

This book is dedicated to the memory of
my dear father-in-law,
Gerald (Jerry) Clubine.
(9/6/1939 – 1/22/2023)
For the almost forty years that I knew him, he inspired
me with his knowledge of the Bible and his
commitment to weekly teaching the Word
in his Sunday Bible studies.


I also dedicate this book to my
Thursday night Bible study ladies,
for inspiring me to dig deeper into Scripture and
build up a knowledge bank of memory verses.
You sisters are such a blessing to me!

## Contents

How to use this book ......................................................... 17
**The LOVE of God** ........................................................... 21
Memory Verses on LOVE ................................................ 25

## 1 John 3:18 (BSB)

 

**The Mercy of God** .......................................................... 35
Memory Verses on MERCY ............................................ 39

**The Grace of God** .......................................................... 49
Memory Verses on GRACE ........................................... 53

**The Patience of God** ...................................................... 63
Memory Verses on PATIENCE ...................................... 67

**The Faithfulness of God** ............................................... 77
Memory Verses on FAITHFULNESS ........................... 81

**The Goodness of God** ........................................................... 91
Memory Verses on GOODNESS ................................... 95

**The Fellowship of God** ............................................... 105
Memory Verses on FELLOWSHIP ............................. 109

**The Perfection of God** ................................................... 119
Memory Verses on PERFECTION .............................. 123

**The Righteousness of God** ........................................... 133
Memory Verses on RIGHTEOUSNESS ...................... 137

**The Holiness of God** .................................................... 147
Memory Verses on HOLINESS ................................... 151

**The Sovereignty of God** ............................................. 161
Memory Verses on SOVEREIGNTY .......................... 165

**The Omnipotence of God** ........................................... 175
Memory Verses on OMNIPOTENCE .......................... 179

**The Omniscience of God** ............................................ 189
Memory Verses on OMNISCIENCE ........................... 193

**The Omnipresence of God** .......................................... 203
Memory Verses on OMNIPRESENCE ........................ 207

**The Aseity of God** ........................................................217
Memory Verses on ASEITY .........................................221

**The Glory of God** .......................................................... 231
Memory Verses on GLORY ......................................... 235

_____

_____

_____

_____

_____

_____

_____

_____

_____

Resources ..................................................................... 221

## How to use this book

Psalm 119:11 says, "I have stored up Your word in my heart, that I might not sin against You" (ESV). That is what this book is to do. With a great yearning to memorize Scripture, but a need to keep it organized and able to reference and use, I created this concept.

Each section represents an attribute of God's character. You'll find a short in-depth word-study on the attribute itself and the concept as well as a biblical basis for including the attribute as part of God's character. Throughout the short study are verses that can become your focus for memorizing elements of this attribute.

Then you'll find a bonus link for each section that leads to a webpage with various sermons that go deeper into each of the topics. Even some of the linked songs have Scripture references. Music is known to enhance memory, so these links are included as well to further build a knowledge of God through His characteristics.

At the end of each section is an area for you to work on memory work about this attribute. You'll notice that the first page of the LOVE section is filled out with one verse and a number of options to assist in memorizing it.

When you add a verse to an Attribute's section, add the reference to the Table of Contents, under the correct Attribute. That will help you organize your memory bank and keep a record of verses specifically about God to help in any situation.

## Learning Styles

The memorization techniques are based on educational learning styles. These styles have been defined after years of study by educational experts. People tend to learn better in a particular way. Many people are visual learners. When they see something, they take it in and commit it to memory. If you're a visual learner, then merely reading your verse might be all that you need. Going further, drawing pictures or creating a single image as a reminder of the verse can cement it into your memory.

Some are audio learners and can merely listen to something in order to have it firmly in their minds. This type of learner should definitely read their memory verse allowed or quote it into a recording app to listen to it again and again. While these two types make up the majority of learners together, another large group of learners have to take action in order to learn well.

These active learners are broken into three parts, depending on what type of movement they need. "Kinesthetic" usually deals with large muscle groups. These learners will often move around while reading through things or speaking on the phone. Listening to the memory verse while running or biking, or reciting it while walking will solidify the verse more quickly.

A tactile learner uses touch to help study or memorize. Writing the verse or its key components, drawing images of the verse, or tracing the words with a finger will help this memorizer succeed. Just a note here –

typing doesn't tend to help with tactile learners as much as writing the words out by hand.

A final type of learner is the oral one. This learner needs to vocalize the words, speaking them allowed. Singing a memory verse will cement it into the minds of this learner.

On the first page of the first memorization section, a verse has been shared, written out by hand. Beneath the verse is a space for the verse to be doodled. This can be done with specific images that can remind you of the words of the verse. This area can also be used by a tactile learner to draw randomly as they listen to the verse being read, read it aloud, or practice reciting it.

Under that is special technique where the first letter and all punctuation for the verse is copied. This mnemonic not only helps memorize, but it can also be a device to give hints about the verse before it is firmly committed to memory.

Strive to memorize word for word in order to be sure you are maintaining the meaning of the verse, but if a word here or there is substituted without changing the meaning, give yourself grace.

Lastly, memorize in the Bible version that you most often use or that is most often used in your church or small group meetings. Staying with one version will help you find the verses quicker when you recall them to mind years into the future.

## The LOVE of God

This isn't the Beatles type from "All You Need is Love" and it isn't simple. It also isn't an emotion, though the evil one has thrown that disguise over it for centuries.

Love is God's chief attribute. From it stems mercy and grace. It is infinite and beyond understanding, and best displayed through the sacrifice of Jesus on the cross. That was an act of pure love. In fact, God always shows His love.

Webster describes love as "a feeling of strong attachment induced by that which delights or commands admiration; preeminent kindness or devotion to one another. Affection or kind feeling."

Notice how all the parts of Webster's definition begin and end with feelings? Emotions? That's not love. Love, throughout the Bible, is an action verb that is shown by behaviors of those who love toward those who are loved.

The Hebrew verb used over and over for God's love is

*Hesed* (*Khesed, chesed*). GotQuestions.org explains that it isn't merely emotion. It inspires compassionate behavior based on love and loyalty toward someone else. The love-actions have nothing really to do with the recipient. And so it is with God throughout the Bible, who loved with His actions again and again to people who were stubborn and resistant to love Him back. Just like we are.

Hesed surpasses affection, friendship, or ordinary kindness. It runs deeper than fluctuating emotions and has the highest level of commitment. Such as is found in some families. It is a love made up of actions. In Isaiah 48:14, 20-21, 62:9-12, and 63:3 and 12, God is providing for the physical, mental, moral, and spiritual needs of His people. He loved them in Exodus, protecting them not only from the Egyptians, but not even letting their clothes get old during their forty-year travels in the wilderness (Deut. 8:4). He loved them through all of the prophets, identifying their need, chastising them for their disobedience as a loving Father, and drawing them back to Himself again and again.

In Zephaniah, He reminds them again of His love, speaking into their future. "The LORD your God is with you, the Mighty Warrior who saves. He will take great delight in you; in His love He will no longer rebuke you but will rejoice over you with singing" (Zeph. 3:17 NIV). And indeed, He does rejoice over his children, both from Israel and those adopted into His family.

God's active love is shown in the New Testament as

well, beautifully portrayed in the parable of the prodigal son in Luke 15. The word love is broken into several types of love in the Greek: e*ros* for romantic passion, *philia* for deep friendship, *ludus* for playful love, *pragma* for longstanding love, and *philautia* for love of the self.

*Agape* is the love that is most associated with God. Agape is the "in-spite-of" love. It loves even when the recipient is unlovable.

God completely forgives us from the sin that keeps us captive, through Jesus' death on the cross that paid our debt. This message of the gospel is rooted in Hesed and Agape and shows God's active love for all people, not only His people of Israel.

John draws God's love up as a conclusion based on what had been seen by His followers in 1 John 4:10. "In this is love, not that we loved God, but that He loved us and sent His Son to be the propitiations (atoning sacrifice) for our sins."

After all that we know about God, we can see His love through His actions and His consistent engagement with people. And it continues with His nurturing of His children, and His persistent reaching to the people of the world who might turn and see His great love.

Bonus Material:

There are a number of songs that speak of the love of God and a dynamic sermon by Dr. Charles Stanley. There's even a short bonus video linked to the page at the following QR code or find it at www.marjilaine.com/attributes-of-god-love.

And here's a great verse that you might consider as a first step on your memorization journey.

*See how great a love the Father has given us, that we would be called children of God; and in fact we are.*

1 John 3:1 NASB

# Memory Verses on LOVE

*See how great a love the Father has given us, that we would be called children of God; and in fact we are.*

SHGALTFHGU, TWW BCCO G; AIFWA.

## The Mercy of God

Mercy and grace walk hand in hand through Scripture. Both stem from love, the deep and unfathomable love that is discussed in the previous section. But mercy and grace are not the same things. They are partners, but just like an architect and a builder, they each have their own purpose to satisfy.

And there's no chicken or egg conundrum here, either. Mercy comes first, borne out of love, and grows into grace.

Webster explains mercy this way: "Forbearance to inflict harm under circumstances of provocation, when one has the power to inflict it." A lot of big words here, but basically choosing not to punish when provoked even though one has the power and the right to punish.

In the ATS Bible Dictionary, it says: "The divine goodness exercised towards the watched and guilty, in harmony with truth and justice."

And the Easton Bible Dictionary simply shares it as compassion for the miserable.

ISB Encyclopedia adds that it is a "distinctive Bible word characterizing God as revealed to men."

The Hebrew word for mercy is *checdh*, meaning lovingkindness. It is described as an essential quality of God in Exodus 34:6-7, Deuteronomy 4:31, and Psalm 62:12.

According to Micah 7:18, 20 and Psalm 52:8, it is God's delight. And Exodus 33:19 explains, "I will have mercy on whom I have mercy, and I will have compassion on whom I have compassion." This makes it clear that God's mercy is given because God wants to give it. Not because the receiver does anything to gain His mercy.

The Greek word is *oiktiermos,* meaning pity or compassion. Paul's use of this word in his first letter to Timothy defines mercy within the character of God. "But God had mercy on me so that Christ Jesus could use me as a prime example of His great patience with even the worst sinners. Then others will realize that they too, can believe in Him and receive eternal life" (1 Timothy 1:16 NLT).

And then in Titus, Paul goes even further: "But when the kindness of God our Savior and His love for mankind appeared, He saved us, not on the basis of deeds which we did in righteousness, but in accordance with His mercy…" (Titus 3:4-5a).

Throughout the New Testament, mercy is often paired with grace. In both of Paul's letters to Timothy and in John's second epistle, the two are extended as greetings along with peace. No one would confuse peace with mercy, though. Peace is a completely different concept. But for some reason, Christians often think of mercy and grace as the same thing.

They are actually different workers on the same project – us. Because God adores us, He holds back what we deserve as the payment for our sin – that's mercy. Instead, He offers forgiveness – that's grace.

So essentially, mercy is withholding the deserved punishment. Grace is offering something that isn't deserved – in this case forgiveness and so much more. Both are wrapped up in the Person of God, as fruits of His great love for us.

Both are given by God. I've heard someone say in the past that mercy is given by God and grace is given by us to each other. That's not incorrect, but it is incomplete. Mercy *is* given by God, but we are expected to give it as well as in Matthew 5:7 and the parable that Jesus told about the unmerciful servant in Matthew 18.

And at the end of the parable of the Good Samaritan, Jesus asked the listeners who was merciful, and then He told them to "Go and do likewise."

So mercy is given by God to us. It is also expected from us to others. And such should be the case since it stems from a core of love.

Bonus Material:

There is a particularly applicable sermon by Rick Warren about the mercy of God. And there's a wonderful song by Elevation Worship on the page at the following QR code or find it at www.marjilaine.com/attributes-of-god-mercy.

And here's a great verse that you might want to use for this topic..

*But when the kindness of God our Savior*
*and His love for mankind appeared,*
*He saved us, not on the basis of deeds*
*which we did in righteousness,*
*but in accordance with His mercy,*
*by the washing of regeneration and renewing*
*by the Holy Spirit.*

Titus 3:4-5

# Memory Verses on MERCY

## The Grace of God

Webster defines grace as "divine favor toward man; the mercy of God as distinguished from His justice; divine love or pardon; a state of acceptance with God. The prerogative of mercy exercised by the judge or supervising figure."

While mercy is defined as not receiving a punishment that is deserved, grace goes a step further. And frankly, it's inconceivable.

Grace is beyond pardon. It is the offering of an amazing gift that we not only don't deserve, we can't possibly deserve it no matter what.

As love is the instigator of mercy, it is perfected in grace.

In Hebrew, the word *chen* means favor when given or *techinnah* as a supplication for favor, or asking for favor.

Psalm 84:11 uses chen in its description of God. "For

the LORD God is a sun and shield; the LORD gives grace and glory; He withholds no good thing from those who walk with integrity."

The Greek word is *charis*. The word charisma, meaning gracefulness, comes from this root. In Luke 4:22, charis is also used for the word charm. And then in Luke 17:09, it denotes gratitude. In 1 Corinthians16:3 and 2 Corinthians 8:19, it is a donation from the Corinthian church to the believers in Jerusalem. A gift to them that they didn't ask for and wasn't entitled to have.

It is the same in the case of God's grace. It is favor that is undeserved. Romans 11:6 says, "If it is by grace, it is no more of works: otherwise grace is no more grace" (ASV).

The International Standard Bible Encyclopedia puts it this way. "Grace in this sense is an attitude on God's part that proceeds entirely from within Himself and is conditional in no way by anything in the objects of His favor."

"Amazing Grace, how sweet the sound that saved a wretch like me." The beautiful words of a crusty old seaman are as much a poignant reflection of a life changed today as they were 244 years ago for a slave-trader-turned-evangelist. We've sung the song all of our lives, or at least heard it. It's easy to gloss over the words, especially the word grace. Its many uses have watered down the power of this word.

- It's the name of one of my oldest daughter's

high school friends.
- It was what my mom practiced with a book on top of her head.
- It was what we said before dinner.
- Graceful was Ginger Rogers, who matched every step of Fred Astaire, going backward and in high heels.
- Gracefully was avoiding an uncomfortable conversation without conflict.
- Gracious was the charming host or hostess who took care of even tiny details.

But none of these comes close to defining the grace that is such a huge part of God's character. The Amazing Grace that we sing about.

After all the word studies and definitions and descriptions, we are left with God, giving grace through Jesus' death on the cross. Grace is the gospel, the good news, wrapped up in one word.

We don't earn it.
We do nothing to gain it.
We don't deserve it.
We can't pay it back.

Grace, in a nutshell, is receiving gifts we don't deserve. And our grandest gift is eternal life with God. It's an effect of mercy with God's great love for us at its root.

Bonus Material:

There is a great sermon by one of my favorite preachers and even a bonus video. And there's a brand new song by Micah Taylor that speaks of God's amazing grace linked to the page at the following QR code or find it at www.marjilaine.com/attributes-of-god-grace.

Try this verse for this boundless attribute of God.

*For by grace you have been saved through faith; and this is not of yourselves, it is the gift of god; not a result of works, so that no one may boast.*

Ephesians 2:8

## Memory Verses on GRACE

# The Patience of God

I'd always heard that patience is something you want to have, but you don't want to learn. I think the meaning is drawn from experience as the Lord tends to teach with practice.

He gives us "patience practice" just like automatic drills that athletes use so that when we really need it, it will be there. The fact that patience is also a fruit of the Holy Spirit living in our lives just gives amply more as we allow Him to cultivate it.

That's meaningful as we think about our own patience, but God's patience has to be infinitely greater to love a people who openly scoff at Him, focus on themselves, and even have trouble with the meaning of the word love. His patience is unfathomable.

Webster defines patience as the act or power of calmly or contentedly waiting for something due or hoped for; a type of forbearance.

I think long-suffering is also a good definition, though

the word is a little old fashioned. The word "patience" itself doesn't actually occur in the Old Testament, though the implication is certainly there.

Many different writers speak almost the same thing about God. In Nehemiah 9:17, He is "slow to anger" in regards to a specific situation. Several of the psalmists speak of His patience, particularly when it comes to withholding His anger, such as in Psalm 85:1-4, 103:8, and 145:8.

Even some of the prophets such as Joel echo the words. In Joel 2:13, God is slow to anger in response to our repentance and slowness of the same.

Perhaps the best description, though, are the words that God used Himself in Exodus 34:6, "The LORD passed in front of Moses, calling out, 'Yahweh! The LORD! The God of compassion and mercy! I am slow to anger and filled with unfailing love and faithfulness'" (NLT).

The Hebrew there for slow to anger is *arek* which is "long" and *appayim* which means nose or face. Sounds rather strange, but the idea is that anger flushes the face and reddens the nose. Being long in the nose or face is an attribute to someone who doesn't get angry very quickly.

There are many words for such in Greek, but most of them refer to patience that people need to have with each other and with God's plan. *Hypomones* is one that is used about God in Romans 15:5, God is called, "The God of patience" in the American Standard Version, but the word there means endurance, steadfastness, and constancy. Most of the more well-known versions have translated it as "God who gives patience or endurance," but the Greek word technically means "of or having" such. Because our God has an infinite amount, proven by the fact that people are still on Earth, He can give it to us generously, knowing that we desperately need it.

In 1 Corinthians 13:4, patience is the first attribute of love. Since God is love itself (1 John 4:16), then patience is also an attribute of God. And He has shown an inexhaustive supply of it!

Paul speaks of it as well in Romans 2:4. "Don't you see how wonderfully kind, tolerant, and patient God is with you? Does this mean nothing to you? Can't you see that His kindness is intended to turn you from your sin?" (NLT). I especially like this version because I can be a little thick headed at times.

He is patient for us to come to Him. Matthew 18:14 reveals that He doesn't want to see anyone die. And in 1 Peter 3:9, this is stated again. "The Lord is not slow about His promises, as some count slowness, but is patient toward you, not willing for any to perish, but for all to come to repentance."

And He's willing to wait for those who will turn and believe in Him and have life. How blessed we are to have a Heavenly Father who not only treats us with such kindness, mercy, and patience, but One who lovingly teaches us to behave in the same way.

Bonus Material:

There is an interesting podcast, a bonus video, and one popular song by Tasha Layton linked to the page from this QR code or find it at www.marjilaine.com/attributes-of-god-grace.

And consider this for one of your memory verses.

*Don't you see how wonderfully kind, tolerant, and patient God is with you? Does this mean nothing to you? Can't you see that His kindness is intended to turn you from your sin?*

Romans 2:4 (NLT)

# Memory Verses on PATIENCE

## The Faithfulness of God

Faithfulness is as much a part of God's character as His mercy and grace. He keeps His promises – all of them. They may not always look the way we expect, but then our God is so much bigger than we can imagine.

The ATS Bible Dictionary defines faithfulness as "an infinite attribute of Jehovah," giving confidence to those who believe His Word and rely on His promises. And because He is true to His promises, it also gives despair to those who doubt His Word and ignore His warnings.

The International Standard Bible Encyclopedia considers it "part of God's ethical nature, it defines the constancy that God shows in His relationship with humankind, particularly with His people." He is unchangeable in His goodness and worthy of our trust to keep His covenant promises.

The Hebrew word for faithfulness is *emet* as used in Isaiah 25:1. "LORD, You are my God; I will exalt You and praise Your name, for in perfect faithfulness You have done wonderful things, things planned long ago"

(NIV). Most often, God's faithfulness is implied throughout the Old Testament rather than directly stated. His very name, YAHWEH (I Am) is part of His covenant and expresses God's unchangeableness especially with regard to His gracious promises.

In Greek, it is *pistis* which means worthy of confidence and dependable. Romans 3:3 uses this word when it says. "What then? If some did not believe, their unbelief will not nullify the faithfulness of God, will it?"

Because God is faithful to His promises, we can come to Him with full assurance as in Hebrews 10:23, "Let us hold fast the confession of our hope without wavering for He who promised is faithful."

It seems so hard to fully trust anyone or anything. Age sometimes becomes experience that every year brings new disappointments and disillusionments. But God's faithfulness is something we can trust and depend upon. In those same years, He has shown Himself faithful in working and blessing in so many ways.

According to John, God's faithfulness is shown in His forgiveness. "If we confess our sins, He is faithful and just to forgive us our sins and to cleanse us from all unrighteousness" (1John 1:9 KJV). And that's just a single example of God's faithfulness to His promises for the people that He adores. We can see numerous promises throughout Scripture that He will complete. He will not let a single one of them go.

I first came face-to-face with the faithfulness of God through a song from 1985 by Steve Green on his album called *He Holds the Keys*. "That's Where the Joy Comes From" was based on James 1:17, "Every good thing given and every perfect gift is from above, coming down from the Father of Lights with whom there is no variation or shifting shadow."

The description intrigued me. Learning that it originated from Scripture drew me in and it became the first verse that I memorized as an adult. I began reading the first chapter of James over and over. It quickly became my favorite, and it wasn't long before I had committed it to memory

The phrase "no variation or shifting shadow" speaks volumes about our God. Hebrews 13:8 says that He is "the same yesterday, today, yes and forever." So the One who spoke to Abraham looked ahead 2000 years to the cross when He said, "And in you all the families of the earth will be blessed" (Genesis 12:3b).

In fact, God looks 2000 years beyond the cross. Abraham is still a blessing to those who are believers in Christ's redemption.

Bonus Material:

Dr. Charles Stanley has a great sermon on the Faithfulness of God, several outstanding songs speak of it, and there's also a bonus video from the BibleProject linked to the page at the following QR code or find it at www.marjilaine.com/attributes-of-god-faithfulness.

God's faithfulness is something we can count upon.

*LORD, You are my God; I will exalt You
and praise Your name,
for in perfect faithfulness
You have done wonderful things,
things planned long ago.*

Isaiah 25:1 (NIV)

# Memory Verses on FAITHFULNESS

## The Goodness of God

What is true goodness? I find I start my prayers with "You are so good." I'm overwhelmed that God actually cares for me. But how can I describe this goodness?

I've heard it described as anything that is done for the good of others. That's pretty profound. A good teacher doesn't teach for her own benefit, but for the benefit of her students. A good doctor doesn't diagnose for himself. He always has the patient in mind.

And so it is with God. Our good, good Father. Every action He takes is for the purpose of building His kingdom which will inevitably be for the benefit of His people. And we can be convinced of that by the actions He's already taken. The great goodness He proved when His Son took our place on the cross.

Like love, goodness takes action when God views His children. And toward those who have not chosen to believe in Him, God still acts with goodness in the form of patience and mercy.

Webster defines goodness blandly as "the quality of

being good." Goodness itself is defined by the actions of being good. By excellence, virtue, kindness, benevolence, compassion, forgiveness, and generosity.

In Hebrew, one word is *tubh* meaning an abundance of goodness. It's used in Exodus 33:19 when the Lord says that He will cause His goodness to pass before Moses. And that goodness is so great, that Moses could only be allowed to see a portion of it.

Then when God does nestle Moses in the crook of a rock and place His hand over him, He passes before him declaring that Yahweh is compassionate and gracious, slow to anger and abounding in goodness and truth. In this case, the word *checedh* was used, meaning lovingkindness and full of mercy.

In the New Testament, *chrestotes* is most often used which means goodness, excellence, or lovingkindness. In Romans 2:4, Paul queries whether the reader thinks lightly of the riches of God's goodness. He goes on to suggest that the one who does take it for granted doesn't realize that the very goodness of God leads to repentance.

When looking at the world, it's easy to get caught up in frustration. So many terrible things have happened and are happening. Many people, whether they follow God or not, might be led to doubt His goodness.

Doesn't He realize what is happening?

- How people are suffering?
- How evil ones are having victory over the

innocent?
- How deceit and manipulations are succeeding in secret?
- How good people, His people, are being persecuted?

"If He's such a good God, then why doesn't He step in and do something about this?"

I confess, there are times I wonder the same. But because He is good, so good, it isn't His will that any should die without Him. (Matthew 18:14) And for the good of those who so desperately need Him, He patiently holds back the wrath and vengeance that He will take, defending His beloved.

And we don't have to worry about the innocent or His persecuted people or the success of the deceitful over the helpless. God cares for those He loves. And Jesus reminds us of this when He said, "Are not two sparrows sold for a penny? Yet not one of them will fall to the ground outside your Father's care. And even the very hairs of your head are all numbered. So don't be afraid; you are worth more than many sparrows" (Matthew 10:29-31).

Bonus Material:

There is a sermon by Dr. Jack Graham, an article from Grand Canyon University and a great song linked to the page at the following QR code or find it at www.marjilaine.com/attributes-of-god-goodness.

Speaking of songs, this verse has been made into a number of them.

*O give thanks to the Lord for He is good;*
*for His lovingkindness is everlasting.*

1 Chronicles 16:34

# Memory Verses on GOODNESS

## The Fellowship of God

I love the verse about God singing over us. It speaks of the infinite delight and deep adoration that He has for us. I'm reminded of a new father watching his firstborn child take a couple of steps.

That's what our Heavenly Father feels for us. And in His delight, He says, "The LORD your God in your midst, The Mighty One, will save. He will rejoice over you with gladness. He will quiet you with His love. He will rejoice over you with singing" (Zephaniah 3:17).

In Genesis, Moses mentioned that God walked with Adam and Eve in the cool of the evening. I cannot imagine, but that is what we are made for. Fellowship with God will be our future. How awesome is that?

Webster defines fellowship as companionship of persons on friendly terms; frequent and familiar interactions.

In Job 22:21, it was an act of reconciliation. "Be reconciled with Him, and be at peace. Thereby good will come to you." The word for reconciliation here is *hasken* meaning to be familiar with or be serviceable to. And the word attached to it with the directive to "be at peace" is *usalm.* It means to be safe, completed, and friendly.

Another verse within the realm of fellowship is: "Many are saying, 'who will show us anything good?' Lift up the light of Your face upon us LORD!" (Psalm 4:6 NASB). While it doesn't use synonyms for fellowship, it implies that same feeling of friendliness. The delight that the Lord has for us.

In the Greek, *koinonia* is fellowship, but most often indicates human connections. However, nearness is *eggizo* when means to come or make close. As in James 4:8, "Draw near to God, and He will draw near to you. Cleanse your hands, you sinners, and purify your hearts, you double-minded" (ESV).

Probably the best verse that shares the desire of God to have fellowship with us is when Jesus was talking to His disciples as the days of His ministry on Earth came to a close. "My command is this; Love each other as I have loved you. Greater love has no one than this: to lay down one's life for one's friends. You are my friends if you do what I command. I no longer call you servants, because a servant does not know his master's business. Instead, I have called you friends, for everything that I learned from my Father I have made known to you" (John 15:12-15 NIV).

We are admitted into an inner circle into the knowledge of God's thoughts through His Holy Spirit. He reveals the secrets of His kingdom to His friends. We can't ignore His directions to obey His commands though, particularly His command to love each other. Through our obedience, we show our love and devotion for Him (John 15:10 and 14:21).

Because the Holy Spirit of God lives inside us, we don't have to wait until Heaven for the amazing blessing of fellowshipping with the Lord. According to Romans 8:15, His Spirit inside us brings about our adoption as His children so we can even call Him, "Daddy."

We are also promised abundant life. In John 10:10, Jesus said, "I came so that they would have life, and have it abundantly." That doesn't mean wealth. Oh, no. Our God is much bigger than that. We are His joy-filled babies as He teaches us to walk in His truth. Can you picture the delight on the Father's face as we trust Him completely with our steps? This is the abundant life we are to be living in relationship with the Living God. It is solely focused on the joy that we have in the growing nearness and intimacy we enjoy with our Heavenly Father.

Bonus Material:

Tony Evans has a dynamic message about Intimacy with God, and there are a couple of excellent songs linked to the page at the following QR code or find it at www.marjilaine.com/attributes-of-god-fellowship.

God created us for fellowship with Him. Here's a great verse to remind us.

*For you have not received*
*a spirit of slavery leading to fear again,*
*but you have received a spirit of adoption*
*as sons and daughters*
*by which we cry out, "Abba! Father!"*

Romans 8:15

## Memory Verses on FELLOWSHIP

## The Perfection of God

It's hard to really grasp the idea of perfection. We might experience a taste of such when timing aligns with attitudes and the weather to achieve a "perfect" event of some type, but we don't really have a clue of what perfection is.

And even less so when we attribute such to God, who is unfathomable, beyond our scope of understanding. (I think our God is so big that it's beyond us to even understand the scope, let alone Him!) And yet, perfection is at His core right alongside love.

Webster defines perfection as "brought to completeness with no defect, leaving nothing wanting." Not too little and not too much – by nanograms.

The Old Testament seems to agree with Mr. Webster. There are several different Hebrew words that have similar definitions, each with a leaning or a nudge toward a particular situation. One is *shalem* meaning "finished, whole, or complete." In Psalm 18:30, His ways are described as perfect as is His law in Psalm 19:7 using this word.

*Tam* is used throughout Job with the same meaning, but in this case, the word is used about a man instead of God. I think there has to be a shift there somehow. The perfection of a man, even a really good man, like Noah or Job – blameless – can't come anywhere near to the perfection of God Himself.

In the New Testament, the Greek word *teleios* is used to mean complete, full, and having reached an end. It speaks of maturity, mostly talking about the journey of believers to come to their perfection as God is perfect. (Matthew 5:48, 19:21) In Luke 13:32, Jesus uses the word *teleioo* when He says, "The third day I am perfected."

That same word is used as Jesus is praying that God will grow His disciples and those following Him. That they will be "made perfect in one" that the world will know that God loves them. The word itself has the implications of completeness, reaching the ideal and establishing the best possible outcome.

In Matthew 5:48, at first seems to be a command to be perfect as our Heavenly Father is perfect. The verse for decades has been a conundrum to me. It seems an impossible task. But there are two ways of looking at it.

First through the verbs that are translated in the verse. The verb there is translated through the different versions as "be, shall be, must be, to be, and will be." I can't help but wonder if this is a dual meaning type of verse as something to strive for with the assurance that eventually we will reach that perfection, that completeness.

The second way I looked at that was through the context. It follows a sort of changing of the guard. The old tradition was to treat others with the same behavior that they used. If they were aggressive, it was expected that one should be aggressive in return.

But Jesus commanded that we love them with actions even if they aren't kind. He charges His followers to use the same mercy and grace, stemming from great love, that God uses toward us. And in actively loving others, we are acting in the same perfection, the same completeness, that God shows us constantly.

In attempting to contemplate that, from my perspective of living in the constancy of incompleteness, I find utter failure. It is beyond my ability to understand even a glimpse of that type of perfection.

But the very fact that true perfection is impossible to understand blends it *perfectly* into the fabric of God's character.

Bonus Material:

God's perfection is shown in a number of ways through Scripture and through our lives. Louie Giglio speaks on His perfection as a Father and Steven Curtis Chapman sings of His perfect strength in videos linked to the page at the following QR code or find it at www.marjilaine.com/attributes-of-god-perfetion.

Here's a verse to remember about God's perfection.

*As for God, His way is blameless;*
*The word of the LORD is refined;*
*He is a shield to all who take refuge in Him.*

Psalm 18:30

# Memory Verses on PERFECTION

## The Righteousness of God

God's righteousness connects with His perfection, but it has elements of justice within it.

Webster's defines righteousness as free from wrong, guilt, or sin. The Lord is certainly free from such!

In the Old Testament, the Hebrew word is *tsaddiq,* meaning just, or *tsaddoq* as to be just. *Yehtsadaq* means "The Lord is righteous." Another Hebrew word translated as righteous is *tsedaqah*, which is a combination of honesty, righteousness, and merit.

Habakkuk 2:4 speaks of how people believed themselves to be righteous. "Behold his soul is puffed up; it is not upright within him…" (ESV). This is speaking of Babylon during the exile of Israel, but it is just as true today. In pride we are convinced of our own truth, our own rightness. In pride we insult and slander and bully anyone who doesn't believe the way they should – the way we believe. In pride, we ignore, threaten, and make fun of those who disagree, cancelling them by our attitudes and influencing others to join us.

But Habakkuk goes on to say, "but the righteous shall live by his faith." True righteousness is living by faith in God. Not fighting for our own beliefs but simply and compassionately standing by God's Word and those truths. And because we are commanded to, doing so with kindness, using active love.

In the New Testament, the Greek word is *dikaios*. It is in conformity with God's own being – to be innocent and without error or guilt. *Dikeioosune* has more of a justice edge to it where God is the source.

We have to be careful not to assume on a righteousness of our own, using justifying hateful words or actions by calling it "righteous indignation." Such an attitude is not from the Lord who calls us to love others as we love ourselves. Attitudes toward others is a great barometer for whether the "righteous fervor" we have is from God or just our own puffed up pride, as Habakkuk said.

In James 1:19, the apostle urges believers to listen more than speak and resist anger, "for the anger of man does not attain the righteousness of God." So much for "righteous indignation."

The same words in both Greek and Hebrew are used for the concept of justice. Justice seems to have an element of judgment involved. An evaluation, but it can only be accomplished by someone with a greater righteousness. Clearly, God alone has the required amount to make any judgments and thus, only He is truly just.

In Romans 2:11, Paul discusses God's justice. He compares the goodness that God shows to His children with the "severity" or justice that will be given to those who refuse to believe in Him.

And in Romans 3:20, he says, "For by the law shall no man be justified," or made right with God. The law only shows the standard – what people should avoid or guard against. Since humans are incapable of maintaining the perfection required, God sent Jesus as payment, once for all, allowing humankind to be able to wear the righteousness of the Savior.

Paul's letter to the Corinthians makes the restoration of humanity clear. "God made Him who had no sin to be sin for us, so that in Him we might become the righteousness of God" (2 Cor. 5:21).

God's righteousness is so far beyond us that we can't even conceive of it. And this is why Jesus came. John gives the perfect example of it. "If we confess our sins, He is faithful and just to forgive us our sins and cleanse us from all unrighteousness" (1 John 1:9).

The law declares that the wages of sin is death. Jesus, perfect and without sin, took that death that sinful humanity deserved, satisfying the debt of sin. So with our repentance, justice reigns. God is faithful to stand by His word and satisfy our sin-debt by Christ's sacrifice.

Videos:

Bonus Material:

There are a number of videos including one from Tony Evans as well as a bonus video by the BibleProject and a favorite song by Hillsong Worship linked to the page at the following QR code or find it at www.marjilaine.com/attributes-of-god-righteousness.

One of my favorite verses about God's righteousness.

*This you know, my beloved brethren.*
*But everyone must be quick to hear,*
*slow to speak and slow to anger;*
*for the anger of man does not achieve*
*the righteousness of God.*

James 1:19-20 (NASB95)

# Memory Verses on RIGHTEOUSNESS

## The Holiness of God

The word *holy* has deep religious connotations. Used often in hymns as a praise word, not to mention in Isaiah 6:3 and Revelation 4:8, the word almost loses its context.

In the same realm as Hallelujah and Hosanna, *Holy* is a word that is often used and seldom fully understood. Hallelujah or Alleluia is defined in Hebrew as "Praise ye the Lord" and it is a word of focused praise. Hosanna, on the other hand, is not so much a word of praise as it is a plea. "Oh, save!" Yet both are used interchangeably.

Holy seems to fall into the same category, but it has elements of both Hallelujah – as a praise word, and Hosanna – not as a plea in this case, but a statement of fact.

Even Webster's dictionary describes it as a type of perfection. It describes holy as the state or quality of perfect moral integrity, purity, sanctity, and innocence. And the word holds all of those connotations, but there is more to it.

The holiness of God reaches a deeper level. Likely that is why in Revelation, the four living creatures speak the word three times. In Hebrew, there is no comparative suffix like there is in English (like: big, bigger, and biggest). So in Hebrew, they repeat adjectives to show comparison. Sort of like repeating an exclamation point in a text to show more excitement. Holy, holy, holy would be the equivalent of *the holiest.*

This sets God apart from regular "holy." And in fact, the word itself, unlike Webster's dictionary, means set apart.

The Hebrew word for holy is *qadhesh* which means "to be set apart." God declares Himself as holy in Leviticus 19:2, stating that, "You shall be holy, for I the LORD your God am holy." In this case, the set-apart-ness of believers deals with our hearts and actions. God's ethical holiness falls on His believers.

There is a difference between the way that believers or Israel are set apart. Even the sanctification of God's children doesn't reach the level of Holy God. The holiness of His people is more of an ethical type of holiness. Separated from our sin and keeping ourselves separate from future transgressions. We are "a holy nation" (1 Peter 2:9). Set apart from the world to worship God, serve, follow, and obey Him. And the filling with His Spirit confirms us in this special group. That we are sent into the world, but we're "not of the world" (John 15:19).

God's holiness is also ethical, that He "cannot be

tempted by evil" (James 1:13) at all. But His holiness is literal as well as ethical. The Creator is set apart fully from the creation. Think of it like a sculptor being separated from the sculpture that he has created. Like the author is separate from the book he has written. For instance, C.S. Lewis included in his *Chronicles of Narnia* elements of his own character and convictions. But the man himself was far more than his collection of books. On a much larger scale is God set apart and elevated from the physical realm. Even from His children.

There is no way that we can be or aspire to be literally set apart like God is, but we can aspire to elements of His characters. Qualities like love, righteousness, and patience are indeed attributes that we can work to increase in ourselves, allowing us to stand in His presence with clean hands and a pure heart according to Psalm 24:3-4. Being His "holy nation."

Videos:

Bonus Material:

R.C. Sproul discusses the meaning of holiness as does the BibleProject in a bonus video. There are also a couple of songs highlighted at the following QR code or find it at www.marjilaine.com/attributes-of-god-holiness.

God is set apart, much more than we can fathom as in this verse.

*I am God and there is no other;*
*I am God and there is no one like Me.*

Isaiah 46:9b

# Memory Verses on HOLINESS

# The Sovereignty of God

Most of the time, when set before us, the sovereignty of God is easily understood.

Webster describes sovereignty as supreme or highest in power: superior to all others. Independent of and unlimited by any other.

Sovereignty is synonymous with power, might, strength, dominion, and empire. A "sovereign," like a king, is the one in charge.

That definition, *in charge* seems to be relative, though. I would like to add "in today's society," but history proves that the relativeness of *in charge* spans all of time. The Israelites coming out of Egypt questioned Moses' authority, to their own destruction. Germanic tribes attacked the all-powerful Roman Empire, crumbling it at its very roots. Nomads building colonies in a newly-found land severed ties with another all-powerful empire from Great Britain. Corporal Hitler challenged the authority of his superiors, to the detriment of the entire world.

Today, *in charge* is a relative word. Society tells us that we should be in charge of ourselves, not bowing to the wishes of others. In places where that theory has succeeded, anarchy rules. But even in everyday life, people ignore authority whether it is in their workplace, in the classroom, on community streets, or in their homes. So much so that the term "in charge" stretches from the negative connotations of a dictator to the benign description of an ineffective teacher.

Given all of this background, it's understandable why the sovereignty of God is a tricky topic.

Defined by Wikipedia as "the right of God to exercise His ruling power over His creation," God's sovereign choices are made "according to the kind intention of His will," as in Ephesians 1:5. And in verses 11 and 12, His decisions are made "according to His purpose who works all things after the counsel of His will."

That means His choices and decisions are for His own purposes and delight. That could feel a little scary if we couldn't fully rely on the fact that He delights in us, His children.

"Our God is in His Heaven. He does what pleases Him." Psalm 115:3 explains that God's sovereignty gives Him the power and right to be a puppet master. And yet, His great love rules His actions and attitudes.

The word in Hebrew as used in Zephaniah 3:17 and Psalm 115:12 is *adon*, meaning lord, master, and owner. *Adonai* is the plural of adon and that was first a title of God before it was used as His name. The plural is often explained because God is Lord of lords, but it can also indicate the Trinity of our God.

In Greek, the word is *basileus* which means "a king." In this, it often refers to Christ such as in Revelation 19:16, who is "the King of kings."

According to The Gospel Coalition, the sovereignty of God is the same as the lordship of God, for God reigns over all creation. The major components of God's lordship are His control, authority, and covenantal presence.

While His rule is absolute, because of the elements of His character – particularly His love and intimacy – His control isn't impersonal or mechanical, but it is the loving and gracious oversight of our Abba Father.

How blessed are we that it pleases the Lord to love us. It pleased Him to send His Son to die for us in order to restore a relationship with us. And it pleases Him to fill His Heaven with those who love Him.

Videos:

Bonus Material:

John MacArthur, John Piper, and Dr. Charles Stanley all speak on the sovereignty of God, and Michael W. Smith sings a great song about Him at the following QR code or find it at www.marjilaine.com/attributes-of-god-sovereignty.

God is committed to His plans and He will accomplish them as in these two verses.

*My counsel shall stand,
and I will accomplish all My purpose.*

*I have spoken; I will bring it to pass.
I have purposed, and I will do it.*

Isaiah 46:10b and 11b (ESV)

# Memory Verses on SOVEREIGNTY

# The Omnipotence of God

I recently read from a scholar that we do a disservice in teaching the almighty power or omnipotence of God. The man went on to say that it isn't an attribute of God at all, and we shouldn't proclaim it because people pray expecting God to have power to give them what they need and care enough to hear their prayers.

Really? The One who spoke the universe into place isn't all-powerful? He who calls us to His sheltering wings doesn't care enough to hear our prayers? He invites us to call upon Him and He will answer. "He will call upon Me, and I will answer him; I will be with him in trouble; I will rescue him and honor him" (Psalm 91:15). And also in Psalm 50:15, "Call upon Me on the day of trouble; I will rescue you, and you will honor Me."

He holds the hearts of the kings in His hand, beckons the wind, and causes the sun to rise and set. How can we not proclaim Him as God Almighty?

The omnipotence of God piggybacks on the sovereignty of our Father. While the word itself doesn't occur in Scripture, it can be seen throughout the Bible with descriptions of His strength and might.

Webster defines it as unlimited or universal power. The root of the word is used in Revelation 19:6 (NKJV). "Alleluia! For the Lord God omnipotent reigns!"

In Hebrew, no variation of the word is used at all, but omnipotence is indicated by the names of God.

- *Yahweh tsebha'oth* is the God of Hosts. The word *hosts* here isn't a choir of pretty angels. The heavenly hosts are warriors – battle ready – and God is the ultimate general.

- *El Shadday* or *El Shaddai* is used as well, meaning God of power or God Almighty. Used in Geneses 17:1 when God changed Abram's name to Abraham. God calls Himself "God Almighty." The name is also used in Genesis 28:3, 35:11, 43:14, 48:3, 49:24-25, and Exodus 6:3. This word has elements of power and goes side by side with authority and sovereignty.

- *El-gibbor* is the Mighty God or Powerful God as in Isaiah 10:21

In the Greek, the word is *pantokrator* meaning, "with all might and power." The word also has elements of authority and sovereignty.

That Greek word is translated as "almighty" in a number of passages including 2 Corinthians 6:18 (NASB). "'I will be a Father to you, and you shall be

My sons and daughters,' says the Lord Almighty."

In the same way, it's used in Revelation 1:8 (NKJV). "'I am the Alpha and the Omega, the Beginning and the End,' says the Lord, 'who is and who was and who is to come, the Almighty.'"

There are also numerous verses in Revelation alone that speak of the almighty power of God. Verses 1:8, 4:8, 11:17, 15:32, 16:7, 16:14, 19:15, and 21:22 all speak of God's unequal power.

Ephesians 3:20-21(NASB 1977) speaks of His power in a different way; one that is full of hope. "Now to Him who is able to do exceeding abundantly beyond all that we ask or think, according to the power that works within us, to Him be the glory in the church and in Christ Jesus to all generations forever and ever. Amen."

So, while the specific word *omnipotence* isn't used in Scripture, this element of God's character is identified throughout.

Videos:

Bonus Material:

There are a number of sermons about the omnipotence of God, and one of my favorite songs at the following QR code or find it at www.marjilaine.com/attributes-of-god-omnipotence.

God's almighty omnipotence rings through the Bible particularly in the Psalms, but I love the glimpse of Heaven that Paul gives us in Revelation.

*And the four living creatures,*
*each one of them having six wings,*
*are full of eyes around and within;*
*and day and night they do not cease to say,*
*"HOLY, HOLY, HOLY IS THE LORD GOD,*
*THE ALMIGHTY,*
*who was and who is and who is to come."*

Revelation 4:8

# Memory Verses on OMNIPOTENCE

## The Omniscience of God

The omniscience of God is the root of so much of God's activities, and creates such assurance and confidence in the hearts of His children.

Webster defines omniscience as possessing unlimited knowledge. This attribute is peculiar to God alone. As with omnipotence, the word itself isn't in the Bible. Yet the concept of the supreme knowledge of God is spoken of again and again.

In the Old Testament, Hebrew words are used, such as *tebhunah*, meaning understanding, *chokmah*, meaning wisdom, or *da'ath* which means know or knowledge. In addition, words like seeing, hearing, eye, and ear reflect the knowledge of God just like His arm, finger, and hand reflect His power.

In 1 Samuel 16:7, God explains things to the prophet, "Do not look at his appearance or height, for I have rejected him, the Lord does not see as man does. For man sees the outward appearance, but the Lord sees the heart."

Part of the verse of 1 Kings 8:39 NIV is similar. "For you alone know every human heart." God makes it clear here that He sees and understands things about each person that others can't see.

Psalm 139 goes even further in verses 15-16 (NIV). "My frame was not hidden from you when I was made in the secret place, when I was woven together in the depths of the earth. Your eyes saw my unformed body; all the days ordained for me were written in your book before one of them came to be." In these verses, it's clear that not only does God see the heart and the secrets of others, He sees and understand more about us than we can even fathom about ourselves.

Other verses speak of His knowledge of all things. Job 28:24 says, "For He looks to the ends of the earth and sees under the whole heavens." In the NIV, 2 Chronicles 16:9 says, "The eyes of the Lord range throughout the earth to strengthen those whose hearts are fully committed to Him." Psalm 147:4 says that "He counts the number of stars; He gives names to all of them." And finally, Proverbs 15:13 brings it all home with, "The eyes of the Lord are everywhere."

The real meaning of omniscience in the light of these verses is too grand, too huge to fathom for us. In all of these depictions of God's wisdom and knowledge, it is already part of Him. Nowhere in the Bible does His understanding grow or come by reasoning. He simply knows. As in other elements of His character, God is self-sufficient. He has no need of situations or other activities to help Him come to any understanding. He draws all of His knowledge from what He already has, that being limitless in both time and space.

The New Testament writers echo this truth, as in 1 Corinthians 1:21-25, "For since in the wisdom of God the world through its wisdom did not come to know God, God was pleased through the foolishness of the message preached to save those who believe. For indeed Jews ask for signs and Greeks search for wisdom; but we preach Christ crucified, to Jews a stumbling block, and to Gentiles foolishness, but to those who are the called, both Jews and Greeks, Christ the power of God and the wisdom of God. For the foolishness of God is wiser than mankind, and the weakness of God is stronger than mankind." Paul is clear here that mankind's highest and most brilliant thought doesn't scratch the surface of God's wisdom. And God's most foolish thought (if that is even possible) would still be far wiser than anything human beings can conceive.

Paul continues in the same vein in the second chapter of 1 Corinthians, verses 14-15, "But a natural person does not accept the things of the Spirit of God, for they are foolishness to him; and he cannot understand them, because they are spiritually discerned. But the one who is spiritual discerns all things, yet He Himself is discerned by no one."

How comforting and encouraging to know that not only do I not understand everything, I'm not supposed to. And I don't have to since God, my loving Father has all of that covered.

Videos:

Bonus Material:

I found several sermons about God's omniscience, but my favorite bonus video is the song. It is quite the experience and all are shown on the page linked by the following QR code or found at www.marjilaine.com/attributes-of-god-omniscience.

God's response to Job's questioning lays this all out.

*"Where were you when I laid the foundation of the earth? Tell Me, if you have understanding."*

Job 38:4

# Memory Verses on OMNISCIENCE

## The Omnipresence of God

I can't think of the presence of God without the words of David in Psalm 139 singing through my mind. "Where can I go from your Spirit? Or where can I flee from Your presence."

Even without reading David's eloquent response, my mind shouts a resounding, "Nowhere!" And then I am brought to Psalm 23:7 "Even though I walk through the valley of the shadow of death, I will not fear for You are with me."

Again, God's presence is here. Wherever *here* might be.

Webster simply defines omnipresent as being in every place at the same time. Unbounded by distance.

Unbounded. Webster used a great word there. As human beings, without the ability to "beam" here or there, it's difficult to comprehend actually being in two places at once, let alone everywhere. But I would say that God's omnipresence goes beyond Mr. Webster's definition because God's unbounded-ness doesn't only apply to distances and places.

As with the other "omnis," this word is not used within the context of Scripture, but the truth of the word spreads from the beginning of the book all the way through to the end of it.

"In the beginning, God . . ." (Genesis 1:1). He is there at the beginning of all things. And in John 1:1, "In the beginning was the Word . . ." referring to Jesus. Jesus, as part of our Trinity – our Triune God. Jesus was there in the beginning as well. John states that "through Him all things were made" (John 1:3 NIV). And the third member of the Trinity was in the beginning as well. "Now the earth was formless and empty, darkness was over the surface of the deep, and the Spirit of God was hovering over the waters" (Genesis 1:2 NIV).

And then Jesus Himself states, "I am the Alpha and Omega, the Beginning and the End" (Revelation 22:13). He didn't say, "I was in the beginning, and I will be at the end." He clearly used the present tense verb, "I AM." Exactly what God called Himself when Moses asked for His name. He is currently and has always been at the beginning. In the same way, He is currently and has always been at the end of everything. Not only is God in every place, but He is also in every time.

That's just a little mind-blowing. Neither space nor time has constraints on God. But then how could the creation in any way bind the Creator? Deuteronomy 4:39 specifies this reality. "The LORD, He is God in Heaven above and on Earth below; there is no other."

In the New Testament, Jesus shared a further truth of God's presence in John 14:23. "If anyone loves Me, he will follow My word, and My Father will love him and We will come to him and make Our dwelling with him." Not only does this speak of the omnipresence of God but also of the unique personal involvement He has with those whom He loves: those who love Him with their obedience.

This is not a matter of salvation but a matter of truly loving God. Jesus said more than once that loving Him meant obedience. And this verse encapsulates the culmination of such obedience – to have the indwelling of Jesus and the Father. Other Scripture defines this indwelling through the Holy Spirit – the very presence of God Himself.

As believers, we are "in Christ" according to the first chapter of Ephesians (among others). Acts 17:28 says that in Him (Jesus, the Christ) "we live and move and exist." Part of God's omnipresence also lies in His indwelling of His people. How cool to be part of that.

Videos:

Bonus Material:

A new song and several interesting sermons, including one about quantum physics are shown on the page linked by the following QR code or found at www.marjilaine.com/attributes-of-god-omnipresence.

I love how these verses not only speaks of God omnipresence, but of His presence with us.

*Where can I go from Your Spirit?*
*Or where can I flee from Your presence?*
*If I ascend to Heaven, You are there;*
*If I make my bed in Sheol, behold, You are there.*
*If I take up the wings of the dawn,*
*If I dwell in the remotest part of the sea,*
*Even there Your hand will lead me,*
*And Your right hand will take hold of me.*

Job 38:4

# Memory Verses on OMNIPRESENCE

## The Aseity of God

When I set out to memorize Scripture based on the attributes of God, I wanted to include His God-ness. The fact that He needs nothing else besides Himself. I didn't exactly know how to put it.

Aseity is not a word I had ever used. But as I studied the concept, the word began to come up in the sermons and study guides that I referenced.

Wikipedia defines aseity as "the property by which a being exists of and from itself," referring to the Judeo-Christian belief that God has no dependence on anything besides Himself for His existence, sustenance, and purpose. He is self-sufficient, needing no outside help in meeting personal needs – physical, emotional, or intellectual.

And Webster describes aseity as existing of or by oneself; independent of other beings or causes. Not caused to exist by anyone or anything or occurrence.

Again, we have a word that isn't directly used in the

Bible, yet the concept remains. In Isaiah 46:9 it implies that God is the uncreated Creator in whom everything else exists and continues. There is no other Source of life besides Him.

This concept is also discussed in a conversation between God and Moses. Moses confirmed with God that he was to go to the people of Israel and tell them that the God of their fathers had sent him. But what if they ask His name? "What shall I say to them?" (Exodus 3:13).

God said, "Tell them I AM sent you" (Exodus 3:14). And He explained to Moses, "I AM WHO I AM" (even with all of the caps).

This brings in the immutability of God's character. He is the same yesterday, today, and forever (Hebrews 13:8), and that fact breeds confidence in the believer. All of the pieces of His character have existed in perfect harmony and that won't change. His love, mercy, grace, and forgiveness will always be ready. His justice and power will fight for us. His righteousness and holiness will remain and will wash over us.

The magnitude of this concept is too enormous for me to even dwell on. I realize once again that my finite mind has no capacity for the full knowledge of our God. I can't even deal with this one attribute.

May we never think of assume that we've finally gotten God all figured out. He is so much more, so much deeper than we are even able to go. I think that's where the fear of the Lord comes in. "The fear of the Lord is the beginning of wisdom and the knowledge of the Holy one is understanding." Proverbs 9:10.

Honest awe, a fear of the only One who should be feared, accompanies the realization of just how big and grand God is. Yet not terror, for His divine nature draws us, woos us, by His love for us.

Bonus Material:

There are some amazing songs and videos about God's aseity, particularly one by Louie Giglio that I love on the page linked by the following QR code or found at www.marjilaine.com/attributes-of-god-aseity.

This Scripture section ends with the aseity of God, but the whole of it is so good, I couldn't leave out the first part.

*There is one body and one Spirit,*
*just as you also were called*
*in one hope of your calling;*
*one Lord, one faith, one baptism,*
*one God and Father of all*
*who is over all and through all and in all.*

Ephesians 4:4-6

# Memory Verses on ASEITY

## The Glory of God

The attributes that we've studied in this book clearly define the glory of God. He is wider, greater, deeper, and more profound than we can imagine. He cannot be defined. He cannot be diminished except in the minds of people. And He cannot be fully appreciated since we have no way of fully understanding Him.

A "religion" of sorts that seems to be growing today, although it has probably been around since the tower of Babel, is "Apatheism." An apatheist believes in God or the possibility of God. He just doesn't care about Him.

In light of this attribute of God, His glory, the attitude of apathy blows my mind. And yet, apatheists are all around us, even if they don't know it.

GotQuestions.org on Bible Hub says, "God is the most awesome, most powerful king, and should be taken seriously."

And on DesiringGod.org it says, "The glory of God is the infinite beauty and greatness of God's manifold perfections, God's eternal splendor and majesty."

Webster defines glory in terms of worshipful praise, honor, and renown. I think he missed the mark with this one. We "glorify" God through worshipful praise, honor, and renown, but that's not God's glory. His glory is more than can be defined.

God's glory is limitless. It is part of His very image.

The Hebrew word for glory is *kabad* as in Isaiah 59:19, and it carries a connotation of solemnity and power. Most often it is used in the book of Exodus.

Remember when Moses wanted to see the glory of God? In Exodus 33, beginning in verse 18, Moses asked God to show him His glory. God told him that he couldn't see His face and live, but He put him in the cleft of a rock, and He covered Moses with His hand as His glory passed by. Then, when He took His hand away, Moses was able to see His back. And just being in His presence for that instant caused Moses's face to literally glow. Every time he spent time in the presence of God, his face would shine so much that he began to wear a veil so he wouldn't scare the people (Exodus 34:33-35).

*Shekinah Glory* was the divine visitation of the dwelling presence of the Lord God according to GotAnswers.org. The first hint of His shekinah was the burning bush that wasn't consumed, followed by the pillar of cloud by day and fire by night with which He led His people in the wilderness (Exodus 13:20-22).

In the Greek, the word is *doxa* as used in Hebrews 1:3. In speaking of Jesus, the writer of Hebrews says, "And

He is the radiance of His glory and the exact representation of His nature and upholds all things by the word of His power. When He had made purification of sins, He sat down at the right hand of the Majesty on high."

God's glory is so much greater than simple hymns or worship songs. The term itself has elements of infinity and eternity as in 2 Corinthians 4:17 where it says that "God's glory is limitless." And it even gets better.

Genesis 1:27 "So God created man in His own image; in the image of God He created him; male and female He created them." And because we, as followers of Jesus, are His image-bearers, we can share in His glory. Because He indwells us, we actually carry His glory.

That is unfathomable. And not to be dismissed!

Bonus Material:

I've included a sermon and a final BibleProject podcast along with a final song that puts a perfect seal on this study. You can find them all on the page linked by the following QR code or found at www.marjilaine.com/attributes-of-god-glory.

The words straight from Revelation confirm God's unfathomable glory that we will one day see for ourselves.

*Worthy are You, our Lord and our God,
to receive glory and honor and power;
for You created all things, and because of Your will
they existed, and were created.*

Revelation 4:11

## Memory Verses on GLORY

Much of my information and inspiration came from wonderful websites that encourage research and revelation about God and His Word. I am grateful for the following sources of information, particularly Bible Hub which led to many of the other resources.

BibleHub.com

Webster's Dictionary at Merriam-Webster.com

American Tract Society Bible Dictionary at Studylight.org

International Standard Bible Encyclopedia at Biblesnet.com

GotQuestions.org

Wikipedia.org

TheGospelCoalition.org

DesiringGod.org


Questions or comments? Reach me at www.MarjiLaine.com/contact

Manufactured by Amazon.ca
Bolton, ON